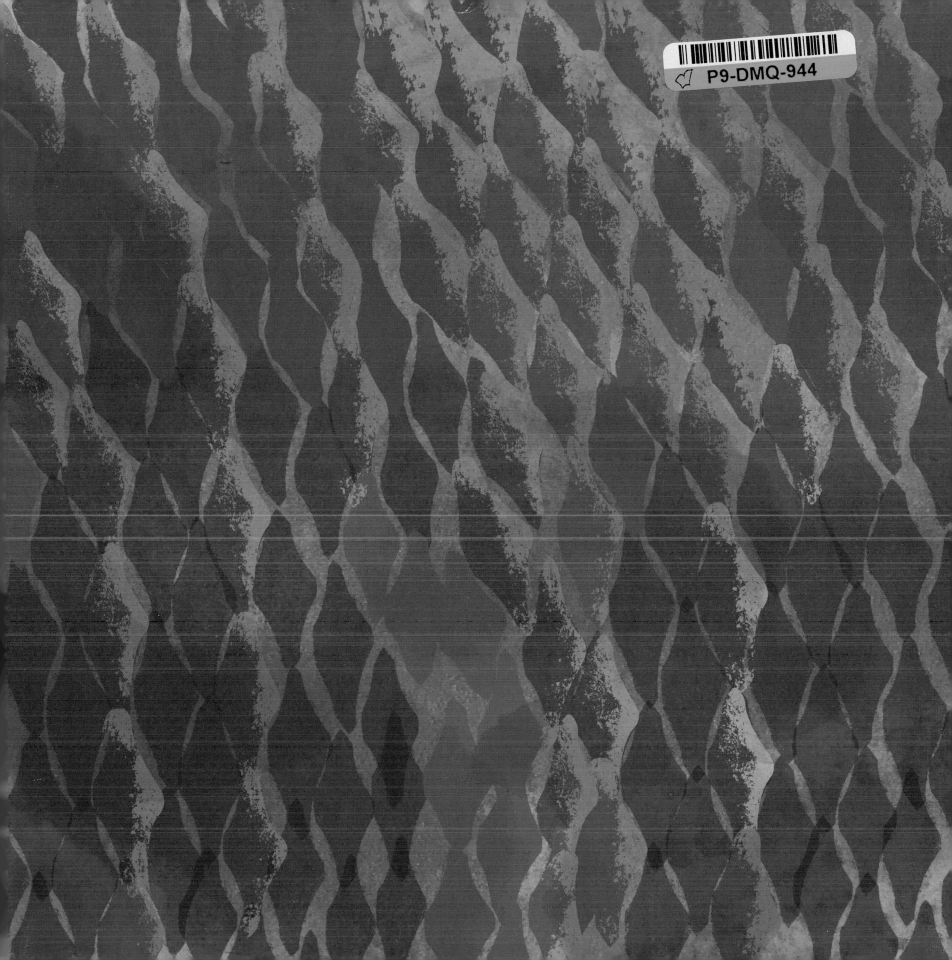

Beach Lane Books
New York • London • Toronto • Sydney • New Delhi

Feathers AND HAIR

What Animals Wear

written by
Jennifer Ward

illustrated by
Jing Jing Tsong

Some
animals
wear
feathers.

Some animals wear hair.

Some animals wear
prickly spines

and roam
without a care.

Some animals wear **armor.**

Some wear a
traveling shell.

Some wear tough and pointy horns that serve them very well.

some animals wear

slippery skin.

Some
animals
wear
scales.

Some wear **Skin**
quite thick—
not thin—
from their noses
to their tails.

Some animals wear **extra fur.**

Some animals
dress **plain.**

Some animals wear **wild hair** that scientists call a **mane.**

Some animals . . .

wear
color...

and change their color too.

But only **one** wears **clothes**

from head to toes. . . .

Meet the animals!

Animals are able to tolerate extreme temperatures, migrate long distances, fend off predators, protect themselves, attract one another, and handle life outdoors without the option of choosing what to wear. At first glance, a wild animal's appearance may seem simple. But there is amazing science behind every part of its physique.

Birds are the only animals that have feathers. Feathers come in a variety of sizes, colors, and shapes, and each type has a specific purpose depending on the species of bird and where it lives:

Bristle feathers: stiff feathers on a bird's head that may protect the eyes and face
Contour feathers: feathers that provide shape and color to the bird
Down feathers: soft and fluffy feathers that trap air, insulating the bird
Flight feathers: feathers found on wings and tails

A **monkey** is a mammal. Mammals wear different types of hair, depending on the species:

Bristles: firm hairs that may be short, medium, or long
Guard hairs: an outer layer of hair that protects an undercoat
Undercoat: short, dense, and fine hair that keeps the body warm or cool
Whiskers: sensitive hairs on the face that provide an animal with information about its surroundings

Porcupines are mammals. They may wear spines, quills, or bristles. In some species, the quills can detach and spear a predator.

The **armadillo** is a mammal. It has a little bit of hair but is mostly covered with overlapping bands of hardened skin that help protect it from predators' claws or teeth.

The **tortoise** Is a reptile. It wears a permanent shell: a collection of bony plates that are fused together and grow continuously throughout its life. Its body is covered in scales. Scales on a reptile are actually overlapping layers of skin.

The **hermit crab**, a crustacean, must find another animal's discarded shell to wear in order to protect its soft, exposed stomach. As its body grows larger, it must periodically discard its shell and find a bigger one.

A **rhinoceros** is a mammal and may have one or two hornlike growths on its nose. The horns are made of thickly matted hair, are permanent, and never stop growing.

A **gazelle** is a mammal with horns, which are permanent and never shed. Both male and female gazelles have horns, but the horns on the female are often shorter. If two male gazelles fight, they may lock horns in an effort to throw each other down.

Frogs are amphibians and most live in moist places or near water. Their skin is soft and smooth, thanks to a gland that produces slippery mucus to help keep it from drying out.

Fish breathe underwater with gills. Most species have bodies covered with scales, which usually grow in overlapping plates. The study of fish scales is called squamatology.

Elephants are mammals known as pachyderms, *pachy* meaning "thick" and *derm* meaning "skin." An elephant's skin may be up to one inch thick on parts of its body.

Polar bears are mammals that wear one of the thickest fur coats in the animal kingdom. Their fur protects them from the cold and wet Arctic environment. Although a polar bear appears white, the hair on its body is transparent and has a hollow core. This structure reflects and scatters all light waves, producing the color white.

Owls are birds, so they are covered with feathers. Although many bird species are colorful, some species, such as owls, have coloring that helps them blend in with the surroundings where they live. Blending in helps them to stay hidden from predators and also allows them to get close to prey.

A **lion** is a mammal. Male lions have long bristles around their head and neck called a mane. Scientists are not sure what function the mane serves, but they believe it may help the lion appear stronger and healthier, features that may attract a mate and frighten off rivals.

The **chameleon**, a reptile, has clear outer skin. Underneath its skin are layers of tissue that reflect light and produce vibrant colors, allowing it to blend in or communicate emotions, such as excitement or fright.

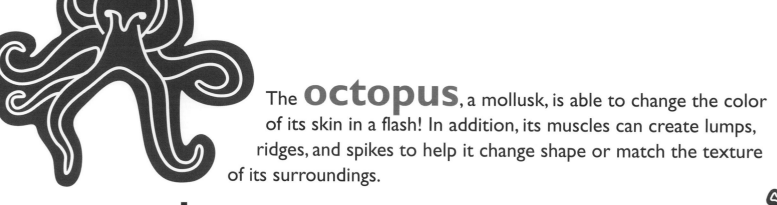

The **octopus**, a mollusk, is able to change the color of its skin in a flash! In addition, its muscles can create lumps, ridges, and spikes to help it change shape or match the texture of its surroundings.

The **sea horse** is a fish, but because of its shape, it doesn't swim well. Instead, it wraps its tail around corals or sea grasses, anchoring to one area. It then will change color to blend in with the background and hide from predators.

Humans are mammals, and we wear skin and hair every day, just like the mammals in this book. Skin covers the entire human body. It keeps our insides in, helps us sense our environment via nerve endings, and protects us from bumps, bruises, and falls. We have hair follicles (spots where hair grows) everywhere on our body except on the palms of our hands, the soles of our feet, and on our lips.

For two women who wear everything well:
my mom, Charlene,
and my daughter, Kelly—J. W.

For Michael, Tien, and Reid,
my favorite creatures to share time
with whether on land or in the sea—J. J. T.

BEACH LANE BOOKS • An imprint of Simon & Schuster Children's Publishing Division • 1230 Avenue of the Americas, New York, New York 10020 • Text copyright © 2017 by Jennifer Ward • Illustrations copyright © 2017 by Jing Jing Tsong • All rights reserved, including the right of reproduction in whole or in part in any form. • BEACH LANE BOOKS is a trademark of Simon & Schuster, Inc. • For information about special discounts for bulk purchases, please contact Simon & Schuster Special Sales at 1-866-506-1949 or business@simonandschuster .com. • The Simon & Schuster Speakers Bureau can bring authors to your live event. For more information or to book an event, contact the Simon & Schuster Speakers Bureau at 1-866-248-3049 or visit our website at www.simonspeakers.com. • Book design by Lauren Rille • The text for this book was set in Gill Sans. • Manufactured in China • 1216 SCP • First Edition • 10 9 8 7 6 5 4 3 2 1 • Library of Congress Cataloging-in-Publication Data • Names: Ward, Jennifer, 1963–, author. | Tsong, Jing Jing, illustrator. • Title: Feathers and hair, what animals wear / Jennifer Ward ; illustrated by Jing Jing Tsong. • Description: First edition. | New York : Beach Lane Books, [2017] | Audience: Ages 4–8. | Audience: Grades K to 3. • Identifiers: LCCN 2016012079 | ISBN 9781481430814 (hardcover : alk. paper) | ISBN 9781481430821 (eBook : alk. paper) • Subjects: LCSH: Body covering (Anatomy)—Juvenile literature. • Classification: LCC QL942 .W37 2017 | DDC 591.47—dc23 LC record available at https://lccn.loc.gov/2016012079